Buddha baby's heart

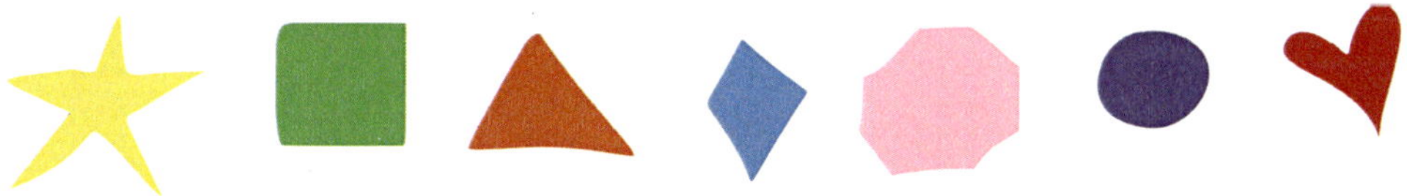

ISBN-13: 978-0-9968660-2-6
ISBN-10: 0996866027
www.buddhababybooks.com
buddhababybooks@gmail.com

Dedicated to Emma & John & Buddha Babies Everywhere

Hello, baby.

Come baby, let us greet the day
with our hearts.

Can you find your heart?

Your heart, like a star,
is a light that guides you.

Your heart helps you to believe in possibilities, even if they are out of the box.

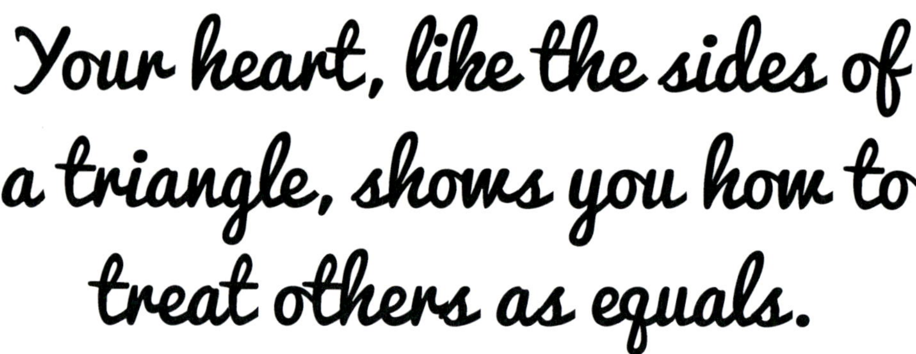

Your heart, like the sides of a triangle, shows you how to treat others as equals.

Some say that a diamond is the most
beautiful gem in the world.
But, your heart shines the brightest
because it reflects your love.

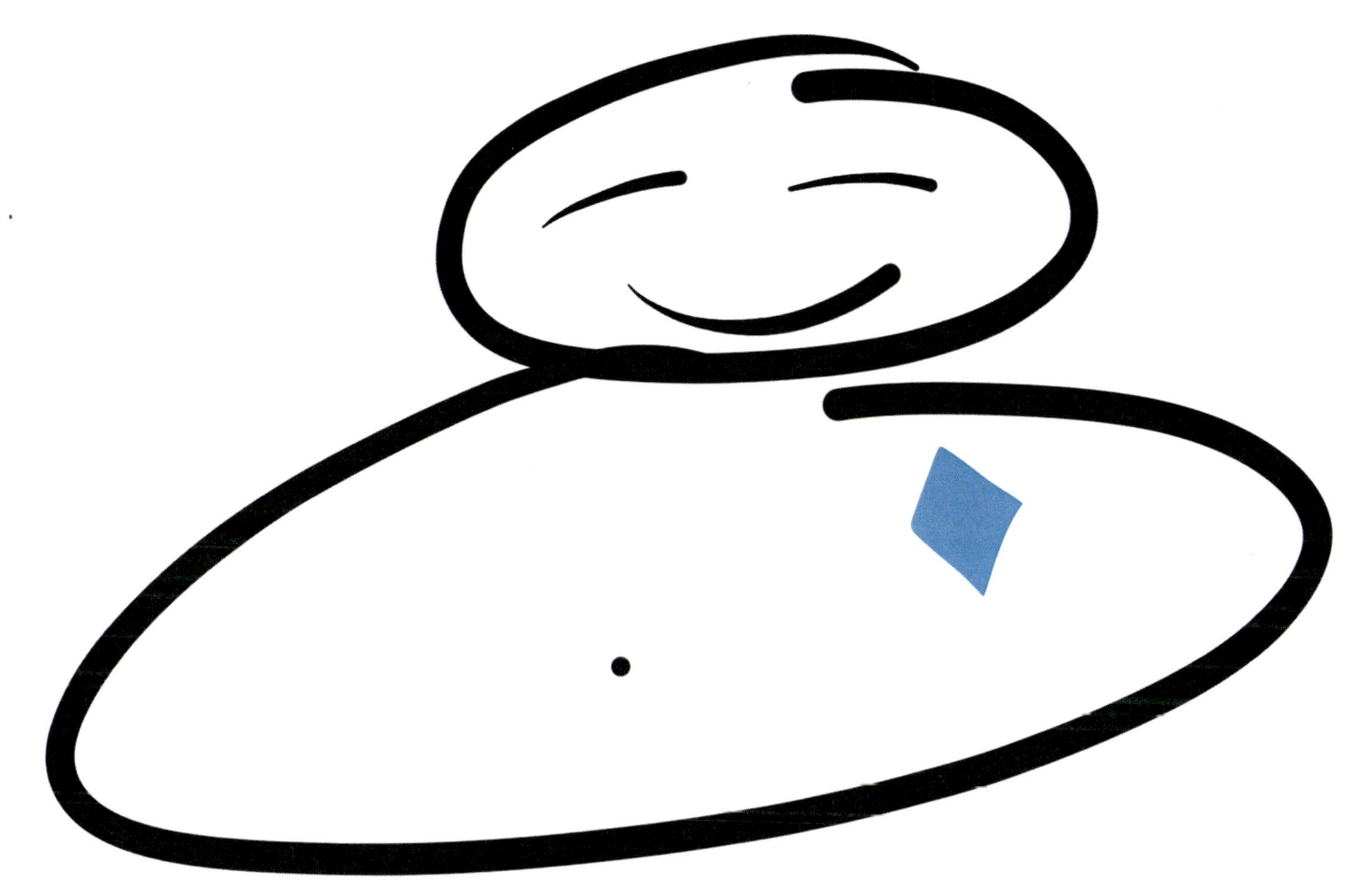

Your heart helps you to see that all things in the universe have many sides.

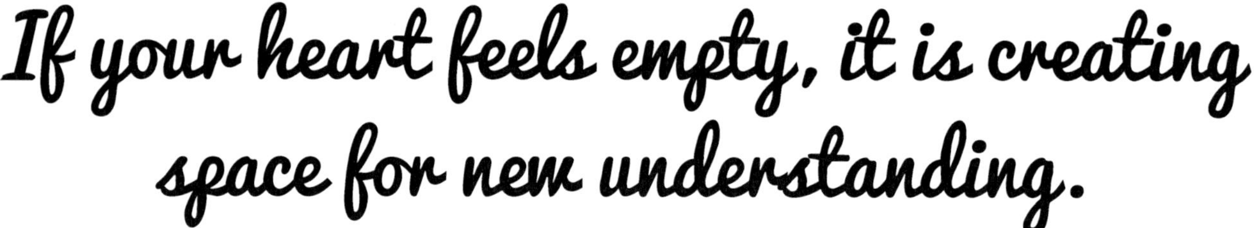
If your heart feels empty, it is creating space for new understanding.

Your heart is your knowing place
that tells you right from wrong.

In you, is where your heart belongs.

The heart that beats in you –
beats for all living creatures, everywhere.

Namaste, baby. You did it!
You found your heart.

Made in the USA
San Bernardino, CA
14 July 2016